Can You Guess What I Am?
Nature

J.P. Percy

How to use this book

This book combines the fun of a guessing game with some simple information about the natural world.

Start by guessing
- Carefully study the picture on the right-hand page.
- Decide what you think it might be, using both the picture and the clue.
- Turn the page and find out if you are right.

Don't stop there
- Read the extra information on the following page.
- Turn the page back – did you miss some interesting details?

Enjoy guessing and learning
- Don't worry if you guess wrong – everyone does sometimes.
- Your 'guessing' will get better the more you learn.

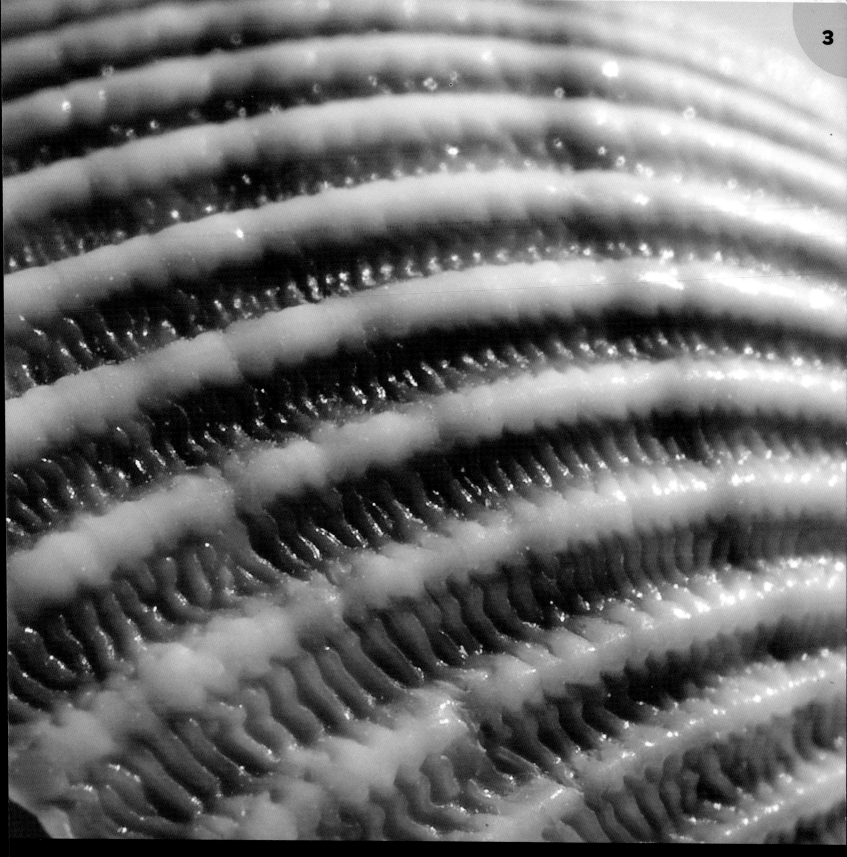

You can find me on the beach. Can you guess what I am?

I am a Shell!

Seashells are the homes of sea creatures such as cockles. The hard shell protects the sea creatures from being eaten!

The wind makes me rustle. Can you guess what I am?

I am a Leaf!

Some leaves are tiny and some are enormous. But they all have veins – like straws – that carry water and food to help the plant grow strong.

I am pretty and delicate and come in every colour. Can you guess what I am?

I am a Flower!

Flowers often have coloured petals. Some flowers have only a few petals and some have lots. They use their colours to attract bees and butterflies.

I lived long ago and can be found deep inside rocks. Can you guess what I am?

I am a Fossil!

Fossils are the remains of plants and animals that lived long ago. A fossil is not the creature or plant but the shape it left in the rock after it died.

I grow on trees with tiny, sharp leaves. Can you guess what I am?

I am a Pine Cone!

Pine cones grow on pine trees. The tree's seeds form in the pine cone. When the cone falls off the tree it opens and the seeds scatter. New pine trees grow from the seeds.

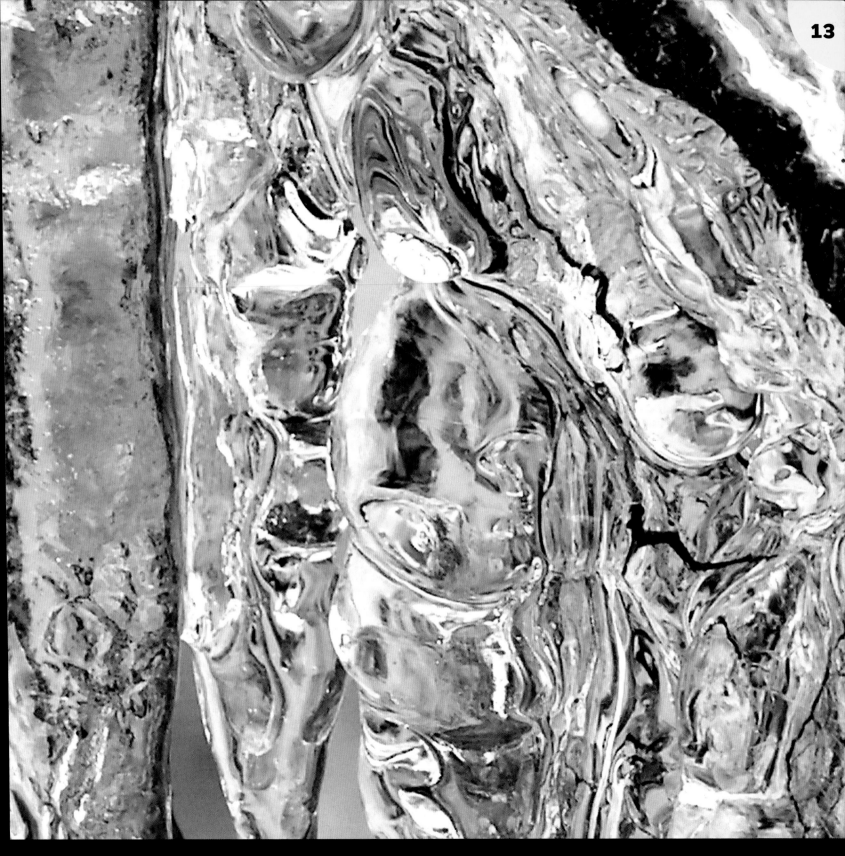

I am cold and glittery. Can you guess what I am?

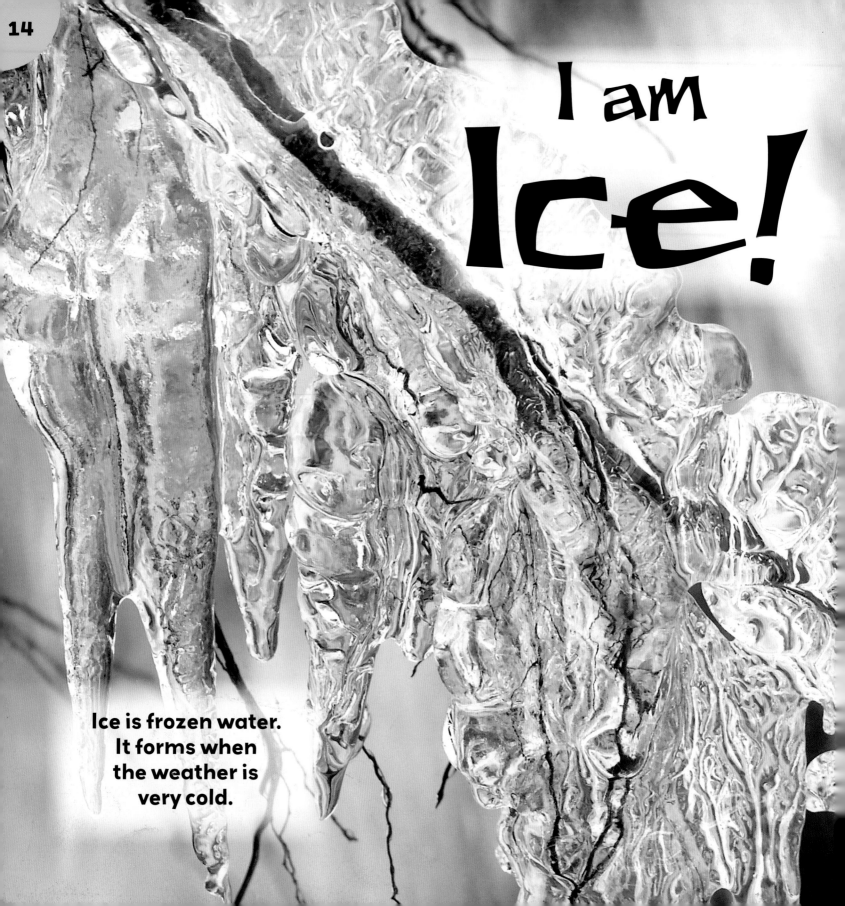

I am Ice!

Ice is frozen water. It forms when the weather is very cold.

I'm round and sticky and catch lots of flies. Can you guess what I am?

I am a Spider's Web!

A spider's web is made of spider silk. It is very light, but it is also very strong. When an insect gets stuck to the sticky threads the spider has lunch!

I am found high up in the sky. Can you guess what I am?

I am a Cloud!

Clouds may look soft and fluffy but they are full of rain. Dark, grey clouds have lots of rain in them. If you see one you may get wet!

I grow tall and you can climb me. Can you guess what I am?

I am a Tree!

Trees grow over a long time. This oak tree is over 200 years old. A tree's trunk and branches are protected by the hard, knobbly bark.

Now try this...

Make it!
Make a picture using objects from nature that you have collected. You could glue a piece of bark to a sheet of paper to make the trunk of a tree.
Use coloured pencils or crayons to draw the branches and leaves. You could put lots of them on one sheet of paper to make a picture of a forest.

Grow it!
Plants and trees all grow from seeds. Cress seeds are easy to grow in an empty egg box. Think about what your seeds might need to grow. How much soil, water and sunlight do they need? When it has grown, you can eat your cress in a sandwich or a salad.

Write it!
Think of your favourite place – it could be the woods or the beach. Imagine you are on holiday in that place. Think about what you might do there – you could go for a walk in the woods or build a sandcastle on the beach. Write a postcard from there.

This edition 2015

First published in 2012 by
Franklin Watts
338 Euston Road
London NW1 3BH

Franklin Watts Australia
Level 17/207 Kent Street
Sydney, NSW 2000

Series Editor: Amy Stephenson
Art Director: Peter Scoulding

Dewey number: 508
ISBN: 978 1 4451 3799 5
Printed in China

Franklin Watts is a division of Hachette Children's Books,
an Hachette UK company.
www.hachette.co.uk